Why a
Do I Pr

Booklets taken from Questions of Life:

Is There More to Life Than This?

Who Is Jesus?

Why Did Jesus Die?

How Can We Have Faith?

Why and How Do I Pray?

Why and How Should I Read the Bible?

How Does God Guide Us?

The Holy Spirit

How Can I Resist Evil?

Why and How Should I Tell Others?

Does God Heal Today?

What About the Church?

How Can I Make the Most of the Rest of My Life?

Why and How Do I Pray?

NICKY GUMBEL

ISBN: 978 1 909309 61 6

Published by Alpha International
Holy Trinity Brompton
Brompton Road
London SW7 IJA
Email: publications@alpha.org

Illustrated by Charlie Mackesy

Contents

Why and How Do I Pray?

Before I became a Christian I prayed two different types of prayers. First, I prayed a prayer I was taught as a child by my grandmother (who was not herself a churchgoer), 'God bless Mummy and Daddy... and everybody and make me a good boy. Amen.' There was nothing wrong with the prayer, but for me it was only a formula, which I prayed every night before I went to sleep, with superstitious fears about what might go wrong if I didn't.

Second, I prayed in times of crisis. For example, at the age of seventeen I was travelling by myself in the USA. The bus company managed to lose my rucksack, which contained my clothes, money and address book. I was left with virtually nothing. I spent ten days living on a hippie colony in Key West, sharing a tent with an alcoholic. After that, with a feeling of mounting loneliness and desperation, I spent the days wandering around various American cities and the nights on the bus. One day as I walked along the street, I cried out to God (in whom I did not believe) and prayed that I would meet someone I knew. Not long afterwards, I got on the bus at 6 am in Phoenix, Arizona, and there I saw an old school friend. He lent me some money and we travelled together for a few days. It made all the difference. I did not see it as an answer to prayer, only as a coincidence. Since becoming a Christian I have found that it is remarkable how many 'coincidences' happen when we pray.

What is prayer?

Prayer is the most important activity of our lives because it is the main way in which we develop a relationship with our Father in heaven. Jesus said, 'When you pray, go into your room, close the door and pray to your Father, who is unseen' (Matthew 6:6). It is natural for human beings to want to communicate with God, and Jesus shows us how. He sees prayer as a relationship rather than a ritual. It is not a torrent of mechanical and mindless words. Indeed, Jesus said, 'Do not keep on babbling like pagans' (Matthew 6:7). Prayer is a conversation with our Father in heaven. So it is a matter of relationships, and when we pray the whole Trinity is involved – Father, Son and Holy Spirit.

Christian prayer is prayer 'to your Father'

Jesus taught us to pray, 'Our Father in heaven' (Matthew 6:9). God is personal. Of course he is 'beyond personality' as C. S. Lewis put it, but he is nevertheless personal. We are made in the image of God. He is our loving Father and we have the extraordinary privilege of being able to come into his presence and call him 'Abba' – the Aramaic word for which the nearest translation is 'Daddy' or 'Dear Father'. There is a remarkable intimacy about our relationship with God and about praying to our Father in heaven.

He is not only 'our Father', he is 'our Father in heaven'. He has heavenly power. When we pray we are speaking to the Creator of the universe. On 20 August 1977, Voyager II, the inter-planetary probe launched to observe and transmit to earth data about the outer planetary system, set off from earth travelling faster than the speed of a bullet (90,000 miles per hour). On 28 August 1989 it reached planet Neptune, 2,700 million miles from the earth. Voyager II then left the solar system. It will not come within one light year of any star for 958,000 years. In our galaxy there are 100,000 million stars, like our sun. Our galaxy is one of 100,000 million galaxies. In a throwaway line in Genesis, the writer tells us, 'He also made the stars' (Genesis 1:16). Such is his power. Andrew Murray, the Christian writer, once said, 'The power of prayer depends almost entirely upon our apprehension of who it is with whom we speak.'[1]

When we pray, we are speaking to a God who is both transcendent and immanent. He is far greater and more powerful than the universe that he created and yet he is there with us when we pray.

Christian prayer is 'through the Son'

Paul says that 'through him [Jesus] we... have access to the Father by one Spirit' (Ephesians 2:18). Jesus said that his Father would give 'whatever you ask in my name' (John 15:16). We have no right in ourselves to come to God but we are able to do so 'through Jesus' and 'in his name'. That is why it is customary to end prayers with 'through Jesus Christ our Lord' or 'in the name of Jesus'. This is not just a formula, it is our acknowledgment of the fact that we can only come to God through Jesus. It is Jesus, through his death on the cross, who removed the barrier between us and God. He is our great High Priest. That is why there is such power in the name of Jesus.

The value of a cheque depends not only on the amount, but also on the name that appears at the bottom. If I wrote out a cheque for ten million pounds it would be worthless; but if Bill Gates, one of the richest men in the world, were to write a cheque for ten million pounds it would be worth exactly that. When we go to the bank of heaven, we have nothing deposited there. If I go in my own name I can achieve nothing; but Jesus Christ has unlimited credit in heaven and he has given us the privilege of using his name.

Christian prayer is prayer 'by one Spirit'
(Ephesians 2:18)

We can find it hard to pray, but God has not left us without help. He has given us his Spirit to live within us and help us to pray. Paul writes, 'In the same way, the Spirit helps us in our weakness. We do not know what we ought to pray, but the Spirit himself intercedes for us with groans that words cannot express. And he who searches our hearts knows the mind of the Spirit, because the Spirit intercedes for the saints in accordance with God's will' (Romans 8:26–27). In a later booklet we shall look in more detail at the work of the Spirit. Here, it is sufficient to note that when we pray, God helps us to pray by his Spirit who lives in us as Christians.

Why pray?

Prayer is a vital activity. There are many reasons for praying. In the first place it is the way in which we develop a relationship with our Father in heaven. Sometimes people say, 'God knows our needs, so why do we have to ask?' Well, it would not be much of a relationship if there was no communication. Of course, asking is not the only way in which we communicate with God. There are other forms of prayer: thanksgiving, praise, adoration, confession, listening, and so on. But asking is an important part. As we ask God for things and see our prayers answered, our trust in him deepens.

Jesus prayed, and taught us to do the same. He had an uninterrupted relationship with his Father. His life was one of constant prayer. There are numerous references to his praying, and in the Bible we read that Jesus often withdrew to pray (eg Mark 1:35; Luke 6:12).

Jesus also says that when we pray God will reward us. We might ask whether it is appropriate to be looking for a reward. Of course there are inappropriate rewards: money for sex is an inappropriate reward. But there are also appropriate rewards. If someone is working hard for their exams, then passing them, gaining a qualification, is an appropriate reward. C. S. Lewis put it like this: 'The proper rewards are not simply tacked onto the activity for which they are given, but are the activity itself in consummation.'[2]

Many of us feel an underlying restlessness or a sense of sadness or yearning, and in my experience, prayer satisfies this spiritual hunger. The reward is that when we pray, we begin to experience God's love for us and his presence with us. The psalmist says, 'In your presence is fullness of joy' (Psalm 16:11, NKJV).

Finally, prayer not only changes us but it also changes situations. Many people can accept that the act of praying in itself will have a beneficial effect on themselves, but some have philosophical objections to the concept that prayer can make things happen, changing events and even third parties. Rabbi Daniel Cohn-Sherbok, formerly of the University of Kent, once wrote an article arguing that as God already knows the future it therefore must be fixed. To this, Clifford Longley, the former Religious Affairs Correspondent of *The Times*, correctly replied, 'If God lives in the eternal present, he hears all prayers simultaneously. Therefore he can appropriate a prayer from next week, and attach it to an event a month ago.'

Jesus often encouraged us to ask. He said, 'Ask and it will be given to you; seek and you will find; knock and the door will be opened to you. For everyone who asks receives; everyone who seeks finds; and to everyone who knocks, the door will be opened' (Matthew 7:7–8).

Every Christian knows, through experience, that God answers prayer. When I started out, I began to pray for little things in my own life. Coincidences started to happen. Then, the more I prayed, the more coincidences I saw. I made a connection and I risked praying for bigger things. Of course, it is not possible to prove Christianity on the basis of answers to our own prayers because they can always be explained away by cynics. But the cumulative effect of answered prayer reinforces our faith in God. I have kept a prayer diary for years now and it is fascinating to me to see how day after day, week after week, year after year, God has answered my prayers.

Does God always answer prayer?

In the passage I have quoted from Matthew 7:7–8, and in many other New Testament passages, the promises appear to be absolute. However, when we look at the whole of Scripture, we see there are good reasons why we may not always get what we ask for.

When we do not confess to God the things we have done wrong, it can cause a barrier between us and God: 'Surely the arm of the Lord is not too short to save, nor his ear too dull to hear. But your iniquities have separated you from your God; your sins have hidden his face from you, so that he will not hear' (Isaiah 59:1–2). Of course, all of us get things wrong, and if this disqualified us from praying, no one would ever pray. But Jesus died on the cross so that we could be forgiven. This in turn enables us to pray. When people say, 'I don't feel I am getting through to God. I don't feel there is anyone there,' the first question to ask them is whether they have ever received God's forgiveness through Christ on the cross. The barrier must be removed before we can expect God to hear and answer our prayers.

Even as Christians our friendship with God can be marred by sin or disobedience. John writes, 'Dear friends, if our hearts do not condemn us, we have confidence before God and receive from him anything we ask, because we obey his commands and do what pleases him' (1 John 3:21–22). If we are conscious of any sin or disobedience towards God, we need to confess it and turn from it so that our friendship with God can be restored and we can approach him again with confidence. God sees everything – it is not possible to trick him by planning simultaneously both the sin and the repentance.

Our motivation can also be a hindrance to getting what we ask for. Not every request to win the lottery, marry a Hollywood star, or own an Aston Martin will get answered! James, the brother of Jesus, writes:

> You want something but don't get it. You kill and covet, but you cannot have what you want. You quarrel and fight. You do not have, because you do not ask God. When you ask, you do not receive, because you ask with wrong motives, that you may spend what you get on your pleasures.
> James 4:2–3

A famous example of a prayer riddled with wrong motives is that of John Ward of Hackney, written in the eighteenth century:

> O Lord, thou knowest that I have nine estates in the City of London, and likewise that I have lately purchased one estate in fee simple in the county of Essex; I beseech thee to preserve

the two counties of Essex and Middlesex from fire and earthquake; and as I have a mortgage in Hertford-shire, I beg of thee likewise to have an eye of compassion on that county; and for the rest of the counties thou mayest deal with them as thou art pleased.

O Lord, enable the bank to answer their bills, and make all my debtors good men. Give a prosperous voyage and return to the Mermaid ship, because I have insured it; and as thou hast said that the days of the wicked are but short, I trust in thee, that thou wilt not forget thy promise, as I have purchased an estate in reversion which will be mine on the death of that profligate young man, Sir J. L.

Keep my friends from sinking, and preserve me from thieves and house breakers, and make all my servants so honest and faithful that they may attend to my interests, and never cheat me out of my property, night or day.

John writes, 'If we ask anything *according to his will*, he hears us' (1 John 5:14, italics mine). The more we get to know God, the better we will know his will and the more our prayers will be answered.

Sometimes prayers are not answered because what we are requesting is not good for us. God only promises to give us 'good gifts' (Matthew 7:11). He loves us and knows what is best for us. Good parents do not always give their children what they ask for. If a two-year-old wants to play with a carving knife, a good parent will say 'no'. As John Stott has written, God will answer 'no' if the things we ask for are 'either not good in themselves, or not good for us or for others, directly or indirectly, immediately or ultimately'.

The answer to our prayer will either be 'yes', 'no' or sometimes 'wait', and for this we should be extremely grateful. If we were given carte blanche we would never dare pray again. Ruth Graham (who was married to Billy Graham, author and evangelist) told an audience in Minneapolis, 'God has not always answered my prayers. If he had, I would have married the wrong man – several times!'

In my experience, it sometimes seems almost as if God has hidden his face from us. The psalmist prayed: 'How long, O Lord? Will you forget me forever? How long will you hide your face from me?' (Psalm 13:1). At times like this we need to trust God despite the silence. As the psalmist puts it: 'But I trust in your unfailing love; my heart rejoices in your salvation' (Psalm 13:5).

Sometimes we will not know during this life why the answer is 'no'. I can think of an occasion in 1996 when I was playing squash with one of my closest friends, Mick Hawkins, a man of forty-two with six children. In the middle of the game he dropped dead from a heart attack. I have never cried out to God more than I did on that occasion; asking him to heal him, restore him, and praying that the heart attack would not be fatal. I do not know why he died.

That night I couldn't sleep, so I got up at about 5 o'clock in the morning. I went out for a walk and said to the Lord, 'I don't understand why Mick died. He was such an amazing person, such a wonderful husband and father. I don't understand... .' Then I realised I had a choice. I could say, 'I am going to stop believing.' However, the alternative was to say, 'I am going to go on believing in spite of the fact that I don't understand and I am going to trust you, Lord, even though I don't think I will ever understand – in this life – why this happened.'

There may be times when we will have to wait until we meet God face to face to understand what his will was and why our prayer did not get the answer we hoped for.[3]

How should we pray?

There is no set way to pray. Prayer is an integral part of our relationship with God and therefore we are free to talk to him as we wish. God does not want us to repeat meaningless words or religious jargon; he wants us to be honest with him and to say what is on our hearts. Many people find it helpful to have a pattern for prayer. For some years I used the acronym ACTS.

A – adoration – praising God for who he is
and what he has done.

C – confession – asking God's forgiveness
for anything that we have done wrong.

T – thanksgiving – for health, family,
friends, and so on.

S – supplication – asking for certain things
or outcomes for ourselves, for our
friends, and for others.

More recently I have tended to follow the pattern of the Lord's Prayer (Matthew 6:9–13):

'Our Father in heaven' (v.9)

We have already looked earlier in this booklet at what this phrase means. Under this heading, I spend time thanking God for who he is and for my relationship with him and for the ways in which he has answered prayers.

'Hallowed be your name' (v.9)

In Hebrew someone's name signified a revelation of that person's character. To pray that God's name be hallowed is to pray that he will be honoured. So often we look around our society and see that God's name is dishonoured – many people pay no attention to him or only use his name as a swear word. We should start by praying that God's name is honoured in our own lives, in our families, in our workplaces and in the society around us.

'Your kingdom come' (v.10)

God's kingdom is his rule and reign. This will be complete when Jesus comes again. But this kingdom broke into history when Jesus came for the first time. Jesus demonstrated the presence of God's kingdom in his own ministry. When we pray, 'Your kingdom come,' we are praying for God's rule and reign to come both in the future and in the present. It includes praying for people to be converted, healed, set free from evil, filled with the Spirit and given the gifts of the Spirit, in order that we may together serve and obey the King.

I am told that the nineteenth-century preacher D. L. Moody wrote down a list of 100 people and prayed for them to be converted in his lifetime. Ninety-six of them had become Christians by the time he died and the other four came to faith at his funeral.

A young mother called Monica, who was a Christian, was having problems with her rebellious teenage son. He was lazy, bad-tempered and dishonest. Later on, though outwardly respected as a lawyer, his life was dominated by ambition and a desire to make money. He lived with several different women and had a son by one of them. At one stage he even joined a weird religious sect. Throughout this time his mother continued to pray for him. One day, the Lord gave her a vision and she wept as she prayed, because she saw the light of Jesus Christ in him, and his face transformed. She had to wait another nine years before her son gave his life to Jesus Christ at the age of thirty-two. That man's name was Augustine. He came to faith in AD 386, was ordained in 391, made bishop in 396 and became one of the greatest theologians in the history of the church. He always attributed his conversion to the prayers of his mother.

We are praying not simply for God's rule and reign in individuals' lives but ultimately for the transformation of society. We are praying for God's peace, justice and compassion. We are praying for those often marginalised by society but for whom God cares especially, such as widows, orphans, prisoners and those who are lost and lonely (Psalm 68:4–6a).

'Your will be done on earth as it is in heaven' (v.10)
This is not resignation, but a releasing of the burdens that we so often carry. Many people are worried about decisions they are facing. The decisions may be about major or minor issues but if we want to be sure that we don't make a mistake we need to pray, 'Your will be done.' The psalmist says, 'Commit your way to the Lord; trust in him and he will act' (Psalm 37:5, RSV). For example, if you are praying about whether a relationship is right, you might pray, 'If this relationship is wrong, I pray that you stop it. If it is right I pray that nothing will stop it.'

Then, having committed it to the Lord, you can trust him and wait for him to act.

'Give us today our daily bread' (v.11)

Some have suggested that Jesus meant the spiritual bread of Holy Communion or the Bible. This is possible, but I believe the reformers were right to say that Jesus is referring here to our basic needs. Luther said it indicated 'everything necessary for the preservation of this life, like food, a healthy body, good weather, house, home, wife, children, good government and peace'. God is concerned about everything that you and I are concerned about. Just as I want my children to talk to me about anything they are worried about, so God wants to hear about the things we are concerned about.

A friend of mine asked a new Christian how her small business was going. She replied that it was not going very well. So my friend offered to pray for it. The new Christian replied, 'I didn't know that was allowed.' My friend explained that it was. They prayed and the following week the business improved considerably. The Lord's Prayer teaches us that it is not wrong to pray about our own concerns, provided that God's name, God's kingdom and God's will are our first priority.

'Forgive us our debts, as we also have forgiven our debtors' (v.12)

Jesus taught us to pray that God would forgive us our debts (the things we do wrong). Some say, 'Why do we need to pray for forgiveness? Surely when we come to the cross we are forgiven for everything, past, present and future?' It is true, as we saw in the booklet *Why Did Jesus Die?*, that we are totally forgiven for everything, past, present and future because Jesus took all our sins on himself on the cross. Yet Jesus still tells us to pray, 'Forgive us our debts.' Why is this?

I find the most helpful analogy is the one given by Jesus in John 13 when Jesus moves to wash Peter's feet. Peter says, 'No, you shall never wash my feet.' Jesus answers him, 'Unless I wash you, you have no part of me.' Peter replies, in effect, 'Well, in that case wash my whole body.' Jesus says, 'A person who has had a bath needs only to wash his feet; his whole body is clean.' This is a picture of forgiveness. When we come to the cross we are made totally clean and we are forgiven – everything is dealt with. But as we go through the world we do things which tarnish our friendship with God. Our status is secure but our friendship is sullied with the dirt that we pick up on our feet as we go through life. Each day we need to pray, 'Lord forgive us, cleanse us from the dirt.' We don't need to have a bath again – Jesus has done that for us – but a measure of cleansing may be necessary every day.

Jesus went on to say, 'If you forgive others when they sin against you, your heavenly Father will also forgive you. But if you do not forgive others their sins, your Father will not forgive your sins' (Matthew 6:14–15). This does not mean that by forgiving people we can earn forgiveness. We can never earn forgiveness. Jesus achieved that for us on the cross. But the sign that we are forgiven is that we are willing to forgive other people. If we are not willing to forgive other people that is evidence that we do not know forgiveness ourselves. If we really know God's forgiveness, we cannot refuse forgiveness to someone else.

'Lead us not into temptation, but deliver us from the evil one' (v.13)

God does not tempt us (James 1:13), but he is in control of how much we are exposed to the devil (eg Job 1–2). Every Christian has a weak area – be it fear, selfish ambition, greed, pride, lust, gossiping, cynicism or something else. If we know our weakness, we can pray for protection against it, and we can take action to avoid unnecessary temptation. We will consider this issue in the booklet *How Can I Resist Evil?*.

When should we pray?

The New Testament exhorts us to pray 'always' (1 Thessalonians 5:17; Ephesians 6:18). We do not have to be in a special building in order to pray. We can pray on the train, on the bus, in the car, on our bike, walking along the road, as we lie in bed, in the middle of the night, whenever and wherever we are. As in any close relationship, we can chat as we do other things. Nevertheless, it is helpful to have time together when you know that you are meeting simply to talk. As I mentioned earlier, Jesus said, 'When you pray, go into your room, close the door and pray to your Father, who is unseen' (Matthew 6:6). He himself went off to a solitary place in order to pray (Mark 1:35). I find it helpful to combine Bible reading and prayer at the beginning of the day, when my mind is most active. It is good to have a regular pattern. What time of day we choose depends on many things including our characters, family life and work patterns.

As well as praying alone, it is important to pray with other people. This could be in a small group of two or three for example. Jesus said, 'I tell you that if two of you on earth agree about anything you ask for, it will be done for you by my Father in heaven' (Matthew 18:19). It can be very hard praying aloud in front of other people. I remember the first time I did this, about two months after I had come to Christ. I was with two of my closest friends and we decided that we would spend some time praying together. We only prayed for about ten minutes, but afterwards my shirt was wringing wet! Nevertheless, it is worth persevering since there is great power in praying together (Acts 12:5).

We were created by God to have a relationship with him. Jesus' death on the cross made this possible and prayer is the way we deepen and strengthen our friendship with him. That is why prayer is the most important activity of our lives.

Endnotes

1. Andrew Murray, *Believer's Secret of the Masters Indwelling* (Bethany House Publishing, 1986).
2. C. S. Lewis, *Weight of Glory* (William Collins, 2013), p.27.
3. For further reading on this subject I recommend Pete Greig, *God on Mute* (Kingsway, 2007).

Alpha

Alpha is a practical introduction to the Christian faith, initiated by HTB in London and now being run by thousands of churches, of many denominations, throughout the world. If you are interested in finding out more about the Christian faith and would like details of your nearest Alpha, please visit our website:

alpha.org

or contact:
The Alpha Office,
HTB Brompton Road,
London,
SW7 1JA

Tel: 0845 644 7544

Alpha titles available

Why Jesus? A booklet – given to all participants at the start of Alpha. 'The clearest, best illustrated and most challenging short presentation of Jesus that I know.' – Michael Green

Why Christmas? The Christmas version of *Why Jesus?*

Questions of Life Alpha in book form. In fifteen compelling chapters Nicky Gumbel points the way to an authentic Christianity which is exciting and relevant to today's world.

Searching Issues The seven issues most often raised by participants on Alpha, including, suffering, other religions, science and Christianity, and the Trinity.

A Life Worth Living What happens after Alpha? Based on the book of Philippians, this is an invaluable next step for those who have just completed Alpha, and for anyone eager to put their faith on a firm biblical footing.

The Jesus Lifestyle   Studies in the Sermon on the Mount showing how Jesus' teaching flies in the face of a modern lifestyle and presents us with a radical alternative.

30 Days   Nicky Gumbel selects thirty passages from the Old and New Testament which can be read over thirty days. It is designed for those on Alpha and others who are interested in beginning to explore the Bible.

All titles are by Nicky Gumbel,
who is vicar of Holy Trinity Brompton

About the Author

Nicky Gumbel is the pioneer of Alpha. He read law at Cambridge and theology at Oxford, practised as a barrister and is now vicar of HTB in London. He is the author of many bestselling books about the Christian faith, including *Questions of Life*, *The Jesus Lifestyle*, *Why Jesus?*, *A Life Worth Living*, *Searching Issues* and *30 Days*.